DIAKRINO

How Is God Judging the
World Today?

ROB COVELL

DIAKRINO

How Is God Judging the
World Today?

ROB COVELL

DIAKRINO:
How Is God Judging the World Today?
Rob Covell

© Printed 2021

ISBN - 978-0-9986539-7-6

Quest Theological Institute

QTI

A Division of Quiver Full Publishing

Cover and inside design layout
Carolyn Covell

All rights reserved.

Printed in the USA

DEDICATION

I dedicate this book to the students at Refuge School of Arts & Innovation. This book's genesis flowed out of a great conversation I had with my students about the ways that God is judging the world and has judged the world. Though much could be written about the subject of divine judgment, and humanity's accountability to God, this book brings clarity to an often misunderstood subject. Many people live in fear and think thoughts about divine judgment and justice that steal the joy of experiencing God as a Father. This book seeks to clarify the judgments of God. To my students: You are amazing young people who "have a hope and a future." The Lord Jesus has called you to recolor the world for His Glory!

ACKNOWLEDGMENTS

I want to acknowledge the following friends, spiritual fathers, and colleagues who inspire me, help me grow in faith, and love me with the love of Christ. I want to thank my beautiful wife Carolyn who is always praying for me, encouraging me, and reminding me of God's goodness. I want to thank my spiritual fathers Dr. David Collins & Apostle Mark Tubbs for always guiding me toward truth and grace. I want to thank my friends, Dr. Gregg Strawbridge, Lay Pastor Steven Navarette, Pastors David & Kylene Frondarina, Executive Pastor Christine Monroe, Prophet Keith Ferrante, and Prophetess Yvonne Camper for being amazing friends and spiritual partners for the glory of God's Kingdom. I want to acknowledge my professors and colleagues at Wagner University who have sharpened my theology and formed me into an active research scholar. I appreciate all of you.

CONTENTS

Introduction................................13

Chapter One: *Cataclysmic Judgment* 17

Chapter Two: *Forsaking Judgment* 31

Chapter Three: *Consequential Judgment* ... 43

Chapter Four: *Eschatological Judgment* 55

Chapter Five: *The Judgment of Hell.* 67

Chapter Six: *How Should Christians See the Judgment of God in the World?* 91

Resources..................................97

INTRODUCTION

I am writing this book in the era of the COVID-19 pandemic. There has never been a time like this in modern history, where every dimension of living is affected. Individual rights and liberties are being challenged, all in the balance of trying to cope and mitigate a plague. In times like these many begin to look at God as the cause, God as the judge of all humanity, and even God as the punisher. As a result, people begin to preach sermons, make podcasts, and social media posts that prophesy doom, destruction, and wild eschatological predictions which will inevitably create fear and rob many of hope. Undoubtedly, thoughts about God's judgment are at the forefront of the minds of many.

If one looks back through the history of

the world, we will find multiple times where plagues affected entire populations and many equated those events as divine judgments for sin. However, if we look into what Scripture says about the times in which we live, what will emerge is a more positive narrative that gives us hope for the future. In times of plague or pandemics, the Church of Jesus Christ is presented with a unique opportunity to model the loving, healing hands of Jesus Christ and represent a glimpse into the Kingdom of God that is the overarching reality and backdrop of life.

In 1527 during a time of deadly plague, Martin Luther, the Great Reformer, wrote: "Those who are engaged in a spiritual ministry such as preachers and pastors must likewise remain steadfast before the peril of death. We have a plain command from Christ, "A good shepherd lays down his life for the sheep but the hireling sees the wolf coming and flees" [John 10:11]. For when people are dying, they most need a spiritual ministry which strengthens and comforts their consciences by word and sacrament and in faith overcomes death." In this letter, Martin Luther exhorts the Church at Wittenberg to determine by their responses and commends those, who by faith do not flee the plague but choose to minister the sacraments, care for the sick, adopt the

Introduction

orphan, and love their neighbors by serving them in their suffering and pain. Martin Luther equates the plague with being a fruit of a world subject to the Fall and death as a result of the Fall.

It is important how we view natural disasters, pandemics, and everything that harms in this world because what we believe about these things either reveals a God of judgment or God who saves, heals, delivers, and is good despite the circumstances in which we live. My prayer for the reader is that after reading this book, you will have confidence, courage, hope, and vision for your life. Our lives are guided by our actions, and personal action reveals what we believe to be true about God. Let us now unlock the mystery of the judgments of God and be thoroughly convinced that we live in the best of times regarding the judgments of God.

Scripture teaches us that there are five judgments of God. These are Cataclysmic Judgment, Forsaking Judgment, Consequential Judgment, Eschatological Judgment, and the Judgment of Hell. This book surveys these five judgments of God and provides a great apology for why Christians should believe that plagues, natural disasters, and bad things are not from the hand of God.

1

CATACLYSMIC JUDGMENT

When we consider the judgments of God, we should correlate them to the narrative of salvation and redemption. The narrative of salvation would have us see that God worked through time and history to reveal truths about His nature and character. Scripture not only revealed God's nature and character but revealed the promise of the Messiah, Jesus Christ, and the great atonement & restoration Jesus gives to humanity. The judgments of God follow this revelation of Messiah in time and history and help us frame our understanding of God's judgments and answer the question; "Is God actively judging the world today?"

The answer to this question sets the compass of our hearts to either fear, to live in hopelessness, discouragement, or live in confidence, faith, and hopeful expectation for the future. The judgment of God is closely related to the salvation and redemption of God. We cannot have one without the other.

If we survey the Pentateuch, (Genesis, Exodus, Leviticus, Numbers, and Deuteronomy) we see are introduced to Cataclysmic Judgments of God. A short list of these judgments is The Flood, Sodom and Gomorrah, God's Judgments on Egypt, The Red Sea Crossing, and Korah's Rebellion. This is not an exhaustive list, but a general list of cataclysmic judgments that happened from the Adamic Covenant to the Mosaic Covenant. There are six covenants that God made with humanity that reveal the timeline and guide the narrative of how God saved humanity from their Fall in Eden and revealed the promised gift of Messiah, Jesus Christ. The six covenants that God made with humanity are the Adamic Covenant, Noahic Covenant, Abrahamic Covenant, Mosaic Covenant, Davidic Covenant, and the glorious New Covenant. These six covenants reveal Christ, His coming, His atonement for sins on the cross, and His coming glory at the consummation. In these six covenants of God, we see a unified narrative and, most importantly, a timeline by which to place each of the five judgments of God. Understanding where each of the five judgments of God belongs on the timeline of salvation helps us understand which of these judgments are active in the covenant under which people live today which is the New Covenant.

The Flood

The first Cataclysmic Judgment in Scripture is the Flood judgment. Genesis Chapter 6 frames the circumstances that led to the Flood event. The movements in the text that unfolded this judgment are 4-Fold. First, demonic spirits corrupted human DNA by joining themselves to women and producing demon/human chimeras called the Nephilim. These unions were contrary to God's design for humanity and the corrupted DNA an affront to Imago Dei in humanity. It was a spiritual warfare strategy of Satan to prevent the Messiah from being born of the "seed of a woman". In Genesis 3:15, the Lord God makes a promise that there would be a Man who would crush the head of the serpent, completely defeat the serpent and restore the dominion that humanity had surrendered to the serpent in the Fall. For Satan to corrupt the human genome was a preventative strategy that would thwart the promise of the Messiah from emerging in history: Jesus

Christ, who is fully God and fully Man.

The second movement in the text is that the Lord limited the lifespan of humanity to 120 years. This limitation restrained the pain that people inflict on one another through their sinful nature. To limit lifespan was to limit damage, pain, offense, oppression, injustice, murder, and any other expression of sin in humanity. It shows us God desires a world that reflects His goodness and God cares about our pain. He also cares very much about the traumas that people afflict on others. It also reveals His patience with the offenders that they may have an opportunity to repent and turn their hearts to Him. Certainly, God never condones sin in humanity or agrees with the horrible things that people do to one another. However, God in His infinite mercy and grace seeks to work providentially in every person's life to save them from the orphanage of this fallen creation and restore them as sons and daughters. Romans 14:12 says, "So then each of us will give an account of himself to God." Nothing that happens in life is separated from our accountability to God. Biblical justice is all things are made right.

The third movement in the text is that the wickedness that was manifesting in humanity grieved God in His heart. This is a very profound statement in the Bible to contemplate. Let's look at the text: Genesis 6:6 says, "And the LORD regretted that he had made man on the earth, and it grieved him to his heart." The Hebrew word for "grieved", *Atsab,* means "God experienced pain, hurt and displeasure that those made in His image would stray so far from His vision for them." It teaches us that our sin moves His heart which then causes a divine response. The Lord created humanity for a relationship with Himself because He wanted to. In His desire for humanity to reflect His nature and character, God gave humanity dominion over the creation and a mandate to expand Eden across the face of the earth. Adam's failure and forfeiture of authority and dominion to Satan not only pained the Lord but revealed a promise that the Lamb, slain before the foundation of the world, would be revealed through human history until all it is restored. Our sin grieves God because He is relational and desires authentic love that is reciprocal between mankind and Himself.

The fourth movement is a contrast that reveals God's commitment to humanity, the object of His love. God's regret is contrasted to the one who found favor in His sight: Noah. Genesis 6:8 says, "But Noah found favor in the eyes of the LORD." It did not surprise God that humanity had sinned exceedingly because the Lord is omniscient. What we see here is God's grief and regret contrasted to His pleasure in Noah (Comforter). Noah emerges as a proto-messianic figure and a type and shadow of the gospel; one man saves the human race through his obedience to God. What we also see is an anthropomorphism where God communicates deep truths in ways that mirror our intellect so that we would understand His heart. Sin and rebellion are contrasted to the hope and future of one man's, Noah's obedience that delivers the human race.

Cataclysmic Judgment the Hope of Redemption

The Cataclysmic Judgment in the Flood begins to frame the purposes of God. The first truth to emerge is that the Lord was defending the bloodline that would produce the Messiah, Jesus Christ. This is important to note because the loss of the Nephilim and the rest of unregenerate humanity is contrasted to the promise of a restored Eden in Messiah. Since the Lord desires authenticity of relationship with His creation, He honored the choices of rebellious and unrepentant pre-flood humanity and they perished in the Flood. This sovereign decision and action of God revealed His promise and the hope He has for humanity that He will receive through Noah. The whole aggregate

Cataclysmic Judgment

of humanity today is related to Noah's family. After Noah and his family emerged from the ark, at least for a time, the worship of Yahweh was re-established, and the knowledge of God and given to every family in the human race. We now begin to see the purpose of Cataclysmic Judgment contrasted to the redemption and promise of the Messiah in the Flood.

The second truth to emerge is that God limited and restrained sin to limit and restrain pain and suffering. Again, we see a sovereign choice in the will of God that brings about good. From our perspective, we might see a worse picture emerge, but from God's perspective, we see His faithfulness in this Cataclysmic Judgment. The Flood stands as an example to humanity that God is committed to redeeming humanity through the Messiah and fulfilling His promises to us.

The good news that follows the Flood is that God promises to never repeat this Cataclysmic Judgment ever in human history. It was a unique one-time event that preserved the genealogy of Jesus Christ, the scarlet thread that runs through the redemptive history on the pages of Scripture. The Lord God gave the signs of His covenant to never flood the world again, that sign being the rainbow. Seven, being the number of perfection, correlates to the seven colors of the rainbow revealing a perfect and complete promise of God that we can trust. The things that follow the covenant the Lord made with humanity after the Flood, is that God again blessed humanity with a mandate to be blessed in Him, prosper, to multiply and cover the earth. The Noahic covenant mirrors the Adamic covenant in that God re-empowered humanity to prosper, revealing His goodness. When we think in terms of the Cataclysmic Judgment of God, we should see the flood as a one-time event, never to be repeated and its purpose fulfilled. This is an important truth to realize as we travel through a brief history of the Cataclysmic Judgments because what emerges is that God's purpose in Cataclysmic Judgment has been fulfilled in history and is not an expression of judgment that God is using in the New Covenant era.

Sodom & Gomorrah

Sodom and Gomorrah is a type & shadow. It is an archetype of maximum rebellion in humanity, eternal judgment, and the end of the wicked who hate God. The saga unfolds in Genesis Chapters 18 and 19. Sodom and Gomorrah are mentioned many times in other places in Scripture as an example of the fullness of God's divine justice and judgment. The archetype of Sodom and Gomorrah as an example of judgment on Israel for covenant-breaking, eschatological and the judgment of hell is extensive in Scripture. It is used in Deut. 29:13, Is. 1:9,10; 3:9; 13:19, Jer. 23:14; 49:18; 50:40, Lam. 4:6, Ez. 16:46, 48, 49, 53, 56, Amos 4:11, Zeph. 2:9, Matt. 10:15; 11:23, 24, Luke 10:12; 17:29, Rom. 9:29, 2 Peter 2:6, Jude 1:7, and Rev. 11:8. This list of Scripture verses clarifies the justification for judgment, establishing Sodom and Gomorrah as the prototype for the end of the wicked, God's final judgment, and God's forsaking wrath towards nations that disobeyed Him in the Old Covenant. Sodom and Gomorrah give us the language of judgment and points our attention to the eschaton, or the Final Judgment, that is to come. Sodom and Gomorrah are a "first fruits" example of the end of the wicked.

There are several movements in the text leading up to the destruction of the cities on the plain, Sodom and Gomorrah. The first is God's dialogue with Abraham, as the Lord and two angels converse with Abraham to reveal God's merciful redemptive ways as he intercedes for Sodom and Gomorrah. Leading up to this dialogue, the Lord God is revealed in a Christophany accompanied by two angels. At this point, he approaches Abraham and Sarah, accepts their hospitality and confirms the promises He has given to

Abraham. He also prophesies the birth of Isaac, and determines not to hide His intentions to destroy Sodom and Gomorrah from his friend Abraham. In Genesis 18-19, we have an example of the Lord's relational ways. His great love and His friendship with Abraham is on display as the God who created the universe condescends and has a conversation with Abraham as a Father and a Friend.

As Abraham intercedes for Sodom and Gomorrah, we learn the truth about God's nature and character. We learn that the Lord will not destroy a city where there are a minority of righteous people. We learn that God speaks to Abraham in words that provoke their conversation and encourage Abraham to probe the depths of God's heart. We learn that God can and will deliver the righteous, using Lot as an example. Later in Scripture, we see Jeremiah's example of equating Jerusalem to Sodom and Gomorrah, but himself being delivered from destruction, the sword, and the famine. Most importantly, we learn that God is good, even in judgment. He is righteous and concerned about the condition of cities regarding their sin, rebellion, sexual immorality, and abuse of the innocent. The Cataclysmic Judgment of Sodom and Gomorrah reveals God's relational ways, His concern for cities, His justice, and His ability to deliver the righteous.

The Archetype of Cataclysmic Judgment has Ended

Since Sodom and Gomorrah stand as the example and an archetype for the eschaton and the Final Judgment of hell, we should conclude that God is not actively destroying cities in the New Covenant era. Sodom and Gomorrah belong to an age on God's redemptive timeline that predates the Law, God's covenant with David, and the New Covenant. The examples of Cataclysmic Judgment in Scripture are active through the Mosaic Covenant, the Davidic Covenant, and end at the sealing of the New Covenant era at the destruction of Jerusalem in 70AD. Though there are many more examples we could use in the Old Testament, the examples of the Flood and Sodom and Gomorrah are enough to teach us that these Cataclysmic Judgments are examples that point us to consider our ways and help us look forward to the eschatological judgment and the judgment of hell. These examples are lessons that have been demonstrated in the salvation narrative, being fulfilled in type and shadow. In the New Covenant age, we do not need to be concerned about Cataclysmic Judgments, but rather be more concerned with redeeming a lost humanity back to God.

Now that Jesus has cut the New Covenant by His blood on Calvary, the Apostolic Scripture of the New Testament presents an era of God redeeming the world through the Church. Cataclysmic Judgment is reserved for the end of this age, but in the interim, the Church is charged as being the preserving effect of nations and cultures. We are the salt, the light, the city on a hill, the Kingdom of God presently present, having both the call and the mandate from Christ Himself to redeem the ethnos consisting of every tribe, tongue, and nation for His glory.

Another dimension of this judgment to consider is the Cataclysmic Judgments found in the Mosaic Covenant. These Cataclysmic Judgments were a condition of the Law. Deuteronomy 28 explicitly contrasts the blessings for obedience and the curses (divine displeasure) for disobedience as the consequences for breaking the Mosaic Covenant. Now that the Law has been fulfilled by Jesus, and Jesus has redeemed humanity from the curse of the Law, the Cataclysmic Judgments of God in the Law have fulfilled their purposes as testimonies for the final judgment of all people. The books of Judges, 1 & 2 Kings, 1 & 2 Chronicles, Psalms, Proverbs, the Major & Minor Prophets strengthen the position that Cataclysmic Judgments belong to the periods of redemptive history leading up to the New Covenant. Jesus even rebuked James and John for desiring to call fire down from heaven in a mini Sodom and Gomorrah event in Luke 9.

Finally, the Cataclysmic Judgments of God in the Davidic Covenant follow the conditional terms that are a part of the Mosaic Covenant. God used overthrows and plagues as a way to discipline David and Israel for these cataclysmic judgments following the conditional nature of God's promises to David and Israel. The pattern of blessings for obedience and curses for disobedience is strengthened as a way of discipline for David and Israel as the Lord works with David for Israel's best. The Apostle Paul wrote in 1 Corinthians 10:11, "These things happened to them as examples for us. They were written down to warn us who live at the end of the age." This verse strengthens the position that the era of Cataclysmic Judgment has served its purpose in God's redemptive history. Furthermore, in Ephesians 2:7 Paul writes, "So God can point to us in all future ages as examples of the incredible wealth of his grace and kindness toward us, as shown in all he has done for us who are united with Christ Jesus." This verse shows us that the New Covenant era of God's redemptive history is an age of grace and stands as an eternal example of God's goodness and grace toward humanity in Jesus Christ.

No one needs to be promoting or believing God is destroying the world or working through Cataclysmic Judgments today. Those that do have missed the unfolding of the salvation narrative of God working through six covenants to reveal Messiah, reconcile humanity, and inaugurate Messiah's forever rule and reign in Jesus Christ's Second Coming. Today, humanity lives in the best era of human history which is the New Covenant age of grace, redemption, and the reaping of the world for Christ from generation to generation as we preach the gospel and wait for the blessed hope of the eternal order to come.

2

FORSAKING JUDGMENT

In the next two chapters, we will look at the modes of judgment that are active in the New Covenant era today. Both of these modes of judgment can be personal or corporate. The modes of judgment that are active in the New Covenant age are Forsaking Judgment and Consequential Judgment. These affect both individuals who stray from the knowledge of God, as well as collectives of people and nations that stray from the knowledge of God. Since aggregates of people are guided by their collective ethos, these judgments are multi-dimensional in their expression in society. We need to understand how God relates to the world around us in terms of judgment in the context of the New Covenant. When we see the world through the eyes of God, we live in greater alignment with His heart. A powerful Christian witness is living in alignment with God and carrying the message of the Gospel to a world that Jesus paid the price of redemption for on the cross. This is the mandate Jesus gave for the Church in the Great Commission found in Matthew 28:16-20.

The clearest New Covenant age apologetic for the Forsaking Judgment of God is found in Romans 1:18-32. Several movements in the text show us that God gave humanity a universal witness in creation. As people groups move farther from the witness of creation, God cannot partner with that people group's sin choices and therefore lifts His hand of blessing from them. Thus, the increase of unrighteousness accelerates and the moral and social fabric of that people group deteriorates. Romans 1:19-20 says, "For what can be known about God is plain to them because God has shown it to them. For his invisible attributes, namely, his eternal power and divine nature, have been perceived, ever since the creation of the world, in the things that have been made. So they are without excuse." Paul clearly states that the creation reveals enough information about the Lord God to direct the hearts of people towards Him. The witness of creation stands as an eternal testimony to the existence of the Person of God and the aggregate of humanity is accountable to this witness.

The Progression of Forsaking Judgment

As Romans 1:18-32 progresses, there is an unfolding degradation in a culture that begins to emerge in the text. The first movement away from God is idolatry. Idolatry in its most elementary understanding is the worship of creation and not the Creator. It can express itself in various forms from images made to represent a god, to sexual immorality, and the worship of the mind. The philosophy of Humanism is a prime example of the worship of the mind because Humanism declares that all truth is revealed in the mind of mankind instead of truth revealed to mankind by God. Colossians 3:5 explains this theological construct: "Put to death therefore what is earthly in you: sexual immorality, impurity, passion, evil desire, and covetousness, which is idolatry." This list in Colossians does not include images of idols, but mindsets that draw the thought life away from God being at the center of the human experience. When people and cultures drift from the worship of the Creator, the exaltation of the human mind veils the knowledge of God and dims the witness of creation. God still stands as the revelatory force of enlightenment for eternity, but humanity chooses to either approach or reproach that witness. In doing so, we invite the Forsaking Judgment of God to emerge in culture.

The next level of this judgment is God giving humanity over to the lusts of their hearts which expresses itself in the objectification and degradation of the body, this includes all forms of sexual immorality. However, we should see that the human body can be degraded in many different ways. Slavery, human trafficking, torture, tyranny, abuse, injustice, oppression, dictatorships, and any other expression that robs liberty and unalienable rights of individuals is a degradation of the human body. The degradation of the human body can be manifested in various degrees and is scalable in its expressions in terms of loss of personal liberty and freedom. Dangerous societies are those that run their course unaccountable to God. These societies have the highest crime, the most murder, the most oppression, the most poverty, the worst health, and the shortest lifespans. The health of a culture is determined by its agreement with God.

The Forsaking Judgment of God continues

to unfold in Romans 1:26-27 where unnatural sexual relations manifest in a culture. This expression of God's judgment is concerning because the grace of God in the procreation of the human race is lifted and the foundation of culture or society is broken, which is the nuclear family. In every culture where people aggregate in numbers, there are seven movers of culture that emerge. These seven movers of culture define and direct the culture into goodness and health or decay and lawlessness in the people group. These seven movers of culture are: religion, family, education, government, economy, media and arts & entertainment. These seven movers of culture are God's design and order for people. God created humanity to live in interdependence with one another for the benefit of the collective. The seven movers of culture pattern not only emerges in Genesis, it is a pattern that is universal in every civilization and epoch of human history. A nation's culture is a metric that can be observed and discerned if that nation is blessed by God or is far from God in the Romans 1:18-32 descending cycle of the forsaking judgment of God. All human history belongs to God's redemptive chronology as it is summed up in Jesus Christ at the end of the ages, so every nation and empire that comes and goes is a testimony to their fidelity to God's natural laws or their departure from

God's natural law.

When the societal mover of religion and family is broken in a culture, the death of the culture begins. The cultural mover of religion guides the moral compass of a people group that preserves the knowledge of God and the cultural mover of the family is the foundation of any people group. When the institution of marriage and childbearing is not honored in a culture, future generations are lost and the power of a people group is weakened. As a culture chooses to stray further away from God, the Forsaking Judgment of God builds momentum as God cannot partner with what is contrary to His nature and character, nor with what is against His design for life.

The Death of Culture & the Invention of Evil

The last movement in Romans 1:28-32 is perhaps the most fearful expression of this serious judgment of God. It is the fullness of a debased mind in the collective culture. Romans 1:28-32 says, "And since they did not see fit to acknowledge God, God gave them up to a debased mind to do what ought not to be done. They were filled with all manner of unrighteousness, evil, covetousness, malice. They are full of envy, murder, strife, deceit, maliciousness. They are gossips, slanderers, haters of God, insolent, haughty, boastful, inventors of evil, disobedient to parents, foolish, faithless, heartless, ruthless. Though they know God's righteous decree that those who practice such things deserve to die, they not only do them but give approval to those who practice them."

The fullness of the Forsaking Judgment of God is an ungovernable people and chaotic culture. These are all the value systems of demonic revolt, rebellion, and malevolency. A culture reflects its collective hive-mind, which reveals its master. It is the corruption of all seven movers of culture and the promotion of the fullness of evil in a people group that destroys a nation. Though the eternal witness of God in creation is always present, the collective movement of a people away from God is the choice of its people. We cannot underestimate the power of the collective mind to either tolerate and accelerate the Romans 1:18-32 forsaking judgment or reverse the Romans 1:18-32 cycle of descent. There are other Scriptures we can point to such as Hosea 4:17, Judges 17:6, and Psalm 81:1-12 which also reveal this judgment of God, however, Romans 1:18-32 is the most descriptive exposition regarding the downward spiral of a culture's movement away from the knowledge of God. Christians in every country in the world should pay attention to the ascending or descending knowledge of God in the seven movers of their cultures because this is the test that Scripture gives us to determine the spiritual health and blessing of a nation. Today in Western Culture, the collective is one cycle away from the fullness of becoming an ungovernable, chaotic, and dangerous society that will be experiencing the Forsaking Judgment of God.

The Christian Response to the Death of Culture

Though this judgment of God is not active or cataclysmic, it is a fearful one because it produces the most dangerous, ungovernable, and poor conditions for people to live in. From Genesis 1:26-31, God designed our experience in life to live well and experience the general and universal blessing of God. God's original design for life, and the seven movers of culture are designed to guide the collective vision of a people group towards God. The Forsaking Judgment of God is the movement of a culture away from Himself. God is a relational Being and God honors the choices of the individual and the collective. All cultures or societies can be evaluated on the descending scale of malevolency described in Romans 1:18-32. It then begs the question, "How do societies heal and move closer to God?"

The answer to that question is found in the Great Commission in Matthew 28:18-20. It reads, "And Jesus came and said to them, 'All authority in heaven and on earth has been given to me. Go therefore and make disciples of all nations, baptizing them in the name of the Father and of the Son and the Holy Spirit, teaching them to observe all that I have commanded you. And behold, I am with you always, to the end of the age.'" Jesus, in the Great Commission (Co-Mission), gives His Church the vision for the redemption and restoration of the nations through the Gospel of the Kingdom. The Gospel is the prescription that not only heals nations but inoculates them from the Romans 1:18-32 descent into the forsaking judgment of God. From the day of Pentecost, the Church has been given the mandate to redeem what Christ had been sacrificed for, which is the redemption of tribes, tongues, and nations. Though the Forsaking Judgment of God is terrible in itself, a loving heavenly Father provided the solution to reversing the curse in His Son and has invited Christians into the work of redeeming nations. The Christian response to the Forsaking Judgment of God is to actively evangelize, disciple, and heal the nations in which we exist. There is no other group in any nation that has been mandated and been given the authority to bring the illuminating knowledge of God to the people around us except believers.

The Forsaking Judgment of God is a constant reminder to the Church in the New Covenant era. Cultural death can either increase or decrease based on the Church's engagement in the seven movers of culture. This means that as long as the New Covenant age is present, there is hope for the condition of the world and the destiny of nations. The advance of the Gospel is the frontline multi-dimensional spiritual warfare waged against the flesh, the devil, and the Babylonian world order to reverse this judgment of God. It is time for Christians in the modern era in which we live, to re-engage the fight to reverse this judgment because we have been called to it and mandated to do it by the very words of our Lord and Savior, Jesus Christ.

The health or sickness in society is either a slow heal or a slow death. It is a generational battle that lives in units of approximately fifty-year cycles of goodness or malevolence. Culture change lives in the long-term vision one has for culture. Many Christians have lost the vision for the goodness and healing of their societies and thus, forfeited the contest in advance. Unfortunately, Humanists have emerged as the ones who understand that the direction of culture is shaped by a long-term commitment to change the culture. When Humanists are at the forefront of a sea of change in culture, it is a clear manifestation that the Forsaking Judgment of God is emerging in a people group. Though there is much to do and culture change can seem an overwhelming task, Christian commitment to our nations will manifest much fruit in the fifty-year cycle of culture change that will touch every one of the seven movers of culture. It is truly a battle between the spiritual Kingdom of God and the god of this world for the destiny of a nation and Christians are the frontline army that is called to victory in Jesus Christ.

As we end this chapter, it is important to note that the New Testament never threatens national judgment or cataclysmic judgment for national sins. God is in the mode of redeeming the nations in the New Covenant age. Revelation 7:9-10 confirms this truth and gives clarity to God's vision for the nations of the world. It reads, "After this I looked, and behold, a great multitude that no one could number, from every nation, from all tribes and peoples and languages, standing before the throne and before the Lamb, clothed in white robes, with palm branches in their hands, and crying out with a loud voice, "Salvation belongs to our God who sits on the throne, and to the Lamb!"

Beloved, let us re-engage the Great Commission and begin to disciple our nations through the redemption of the seven movers of culture. Let us pray for leaders to emerge who carry this vision for our nations and begin to live every day in alignment and agreement with God.

# 3

CONSEQUENTIAL JUDGMENT

The Consequential Judgment of God is related to God's Forsaking Judgment, but manifests in a more personal expression and includes several dimensions that affect the lives of Christians and non-Christians alike. Consequential Judgment applies to the New Covenant era in salvation history and is a judgment of God that lives through our choices. The theological construct of Consequential Judgment is found in several places in Scripture: Gal. 6:7-8, 1 Peter 4:17, James 1:2-3 and Rom. 5:3-5. In this chapter, we will explore each of these Scriptures and expand our understanding of the consequential judgment of God as it relates to our life experiences.

Sowing and Reaping

One dimension of this particular judgment of God is the principle of sowing and reaping. Galatians 6:7-8 is an excellent example of this type of Consequential Judgment. It reads, "Do not be deceived: God is not mocked, for whatever one sows, that will he also reap. For the one who sows to his own flesh will from the flesh reap corruption, but the one who sows to the Spirit will from the Spirit reap eternal life." The sowing and reaping principle operates under the direction of the free will choices of people; either to seek goodness, morality, and move towards God, or seek the flesh (sarx) and move towards lust, greed, sexual immorality, depravity, murder, lying and anything else that is contrary to God's goodness. These two paths are chosen in the everyday decisions of men and women and our futures become the total of those choices.

All our choices are under the covering of accountability to God, and what we have sown through our choices becomes the fruit that is brought forth. The Consequential Judgment of God in the sowing and reaping principle has both temporal and eternal impacts on our lives. This judgment is similar to

Consequential Judgment

His Forsaking Judgment, in that God is honoring the choices of people's hearts. We should recognize that the Consequential Judgment of God is not separated from the providence of God for God is 360° sovereign. God does not exist in a vacuum separated from people, but He is a relational, loving Father. The providence of God reveals His grace in ways that show us He is working through the free will decisions of people to bring about their best and His best for their lives. While Consequential Judgment in sowing and reaping does produce the fruit of either pain or goodness in our lives, it is never devoid of the possibility of God's goodness and grace to change outcomes or work through them in redemptive ways. We do not want to look at this judgment as irreversible or unchanging because God's relationship with humanity is dynamic, authentic and merciful. We do not get what we deserve in terms of sin in our lives because God's kindness and goodness mute and soften the Consequential Judgment many times in the life experiences of people. We should see this judgment as a principle from which real experience emerges, but not a black and white, hardline response from God that is separated from His benevolence.

Consequential Judgment in the sowing and reaping principle is common to every person, not just Christians. It is an accountability to God that cannot be escaped or resisted. The Consequential Judgment of God reminds us that our decisions have consequences, those consequences affect others and ultimately we are accountable for the path we have chosen in this great gift called life. It is very important to note that God is not actively pursuing or punishing with judgment, like the Cataclysmic Judgment of God, but rather this is a judgment from God that simply honors human dignity and respects a person for the choices they make, either good or bad.

Consequential Judgment in the Church

The second expression of Consequential Judgment found in Scripture is in 1 Peter 4:17 where Peter writes, "For it is time for judgment to begin at the household of God; and if it begins with us, what will be the outcome for those who do not obey the gospel of God?" The entire chapter of 1 Peter 4 contains beautiful thoughts and truths about the Consequential Judgment of God for believers. It warns Christians to live in ways that agree with God and for believers to consider the way they are living their lives, empowering them to partner with the vision of eternal destiny to guide their way. It is sobering and beautiful to live with vision, to live a life of simple devotion through prayer, trusting God in the most difficult seasons of our lives. Verse 17 sums up the whole of Chapter 4 with the statement, "For it is time for judgment to begin at the household of God."

The section of Scripture that precedes 1 Peter 4:17 exhorts Christians to not suffer or be persecuted for legitimate offenses against society, but to endure suffering from persecutors of the faith with a good conscience knowing that obedience to Christ and the persecution that follows is godly, true and is the greatest proof that our relationship with Jesus is authentic and powerful. The Greek word for "judgment" in 1 Peter 4:17 is *krima*. It means "a decree, or judgment, a condemnation of wrong, the decision (whether severe or mild) which one passes on the faults of others, the sentence or punishment handed down by a judge in a penal sense, or a matter to be judicially decided, a lawsuit, as a case in court." If we consider the context of this verse, what begins to become clear is that the Consequential Judgment of God towards Christians is a refining process that proves faith, condemns the persecutors, and is an eternal witness that all people are accountable to God, their Creator. 1 Peter 4 ends with an appeal for Christians who endure suffering to entrust themselves to God's faithfulness to

His promise of salvation and eternal life amid their trouble.

The type of Consequential Judgment of God in the Church is not an active judgment of God being harsh towards His Bride, but a real-world acceptance that Christians sometimes endure the worst persecution in their lives, and those persecutions reveal the end of the persecutor, which is a judgment from God. The definition of *krima* (judgment) reveals that God will be the Judge of all and that suffering for Jesus is not in vain nor without hope. This is not the consequential judgment of sowing and reaping, but rather the consequence of personalized evil's hatred of God's people that reveals the persecutor's ultimate fate in eternal condemnation.

The Perseverance of Faith

When we consider suffering and the trials of life as a believer, we should see them through the lens of a redemptive process and an opportunity to exercise our faith. We should never accept suffering as a permanent condition, but we should believe that God will bring good out of it. Suffering in this world is the evidence of a great spiritual war that is being waged on multiple fronts fighting the devil and demons, the flesh, sickness, disease, poverty, and the reality of living in a fallen world that is subject to the corruption we inherited from Adam. Multi-dimensional spiritual warfare takes many forms and manifests in ways too numerous to list. However, the way forward in this spiritual fight for the restoration of all things is the perseverance of our faith. Perseverance of faith is the highest level of resistance to everything contrary to the goodness of God. Perseverance of faith hangs in the balance of the Forsaking Judgment and Consequential Judgments of God.

Two more great sections of Scripture that call us to the fight of the perseverance of faith are James 1:2-3 and Romans 5:3-5. To expand our understanding of the perseverance of faith, we will start with James 1:2-3, "Count it all joy, my brothers, when you meet trials of various kinds, for you know that the testing of your faith produces steadfastness." These verses teach us that all trials are opportunities to find the joy of God. The Greek word for "trials" in this text is *peirasmos*. This word means "an experiment, attempt, trial, proving, the trial of man's fidelity, integrity, virtue, constancy, or a temptation/testing." We can see from the definition of this Greek word that there are manifold expressions of the kinds of trials that a Christian may face in life. In the diversity of these trials, there is joy or gladness (*chara*) that one can find because we are in Christ. James teaches us that diverse trials in which our faith in the Lord is tested produce steadfastness, endurance, and constancy. When we consider the Consequential Judgment of God beyond the sowing and reaping principle, and also consider the testing of our faith, we can see the victory and the maturity of faith that is produced and enjoyed as a result of the trial. This is why James so confidently commands us to see God's grace in our testing and exert faith which delivers us from the trial and experience the diverse ways that God delivers His Beloved.

The next Scripture which highlights the blessedness of the perseverance of faith is Romans 4:3-5. It reads, "Not only that, but we rejoice in our sufferings, knowing that suffering produces endurance, and endurance produces character, and character produces hope, and hope does not put us to shame, because God's love has been poured into our hearts through the Holy Spirit who has been given to us." The Apostle Paul teaches us that there is a process in suffering that God works through to bring about good. The Greek word for "suffering" in this text is *thlipsis*, which is usually translated "tribulation." Its literal definition means pressing and is the metaphor for oppression, affliction, tribulation, and distress. The definition of the Greek word reveals that the application of suffering or tribulation can take many different forms and is not confined to a narrow expression. The cause of suffering could be anything that produces pain or trouble in a believer's life. We may be facing troubling circumstances, but they are not permanent and God will produce something good from them, see Romans 8:28.

Our response to suffering is an invitation to the ascending graces that come into being in the life of the believer as they trust the Lord in their tribulations. The first grace that is produced is endurance. The Greek word for "endurance" is *hypomonē*. It means "steadfastness, constancy, endurance, to stand up in faith and not bend, to be steadfast in waiting for God's intervention." This is the definition of "godly courage" that is manifested in the lives of the Christian martyrs who stood in the face of evil and loudly proclaimed their allegiance to Jesus Christ. The lives of the lion-hearted have turned the course of history, released freedom, and revealed truth. Every Protestant believer in Jesus Christ stands on the hundreds of martyrs who were burned at the stake for being heretics, for translating the Bible into their native tongues, and who fought for religious freedom. Their endurance was our freedom in Christ that we enjoy today, as we worship in Spirit and in truth.

The next grace that proceeds from endurance is character. The Greek word for "character" is *dokimē*, which means "to be found, proved, tested and to be found as a worthy example of the fruit of perseverance." It is an enigma to the world around us when Christians stand above the ashes of life's experience to produce beauty and joyful praise which is the first fruits of the resurrection that we hope for in Christ.

Grace from God continues in the text as hope adds another layer of victory in the life of believers. The Greek word for "hope" is *elpis*. This word means "the expectation of good, the expectation of God's goodness and the hope/joyful expectation of being convinced that God's goodness is the foundation and author of good things to come." This definition describes a state of faith that becomes the witness to God's love being poured out into our lives. The Holy Spirit stands as the internal and eternal witness in our hearts that what we believe is true. Our faith cannot be further tested because the fullness of hopeful and joyful expectation has reached its fullness in our lives.

All these things are important for Christians to consider and meditate on as we explore the topic of Consequential Judgment. The glory of

Consequential Judgment

the New Covenant surpasses all the previous covenants that God made with humanity. Forsaking Judgment and Consequential Judgment are defeated and neutralized by the power of the Gospel and the perseverance of faith in the saints. These two judgments are now in play in the New Covenant era, but they do not ever have to be a permanent condition in the lives of individuals or societies because Christians have the authority, the mandate, and the power to change these things in Christ. We have all that is necessary to engage in the great spiritual war for the destiny of nations that have been bought by Christ's bloodshed on the cross.

4

ESCHATOLOGICAL JUDGMENT

The next two chapters in this book explore the judgments of God that are reserved for the end of the New Covenant era when all things are summed up in Jesus Christ. In this chapter, we will explore the Eschatological Judgment of God. There are four views in Christianity concerning the doctrine of the end times, or the Eschatological Judgment of God. These four views are Premillennial Dispensational Eschatology, Classic Premillennial Eschatology, Amillennial Eschatology, and Post-Millennial Eschatology. This book will not concern itself with promoting an eschatological position but will seek to promote the truth that the Eschatological Judgment of God belongs to a future that ends the New Covenant age. For a detailed work on eschatology that promotes the Post-Millennial view of end times, see my book, *The Revelation of Hope*.

While there are hundreds of texts we could explore that speak to the Eschatological Judgment of God, we will concern ourselves with Psalm 2 and Revelation 19. The doctrine of End Times is complex and in the discipline of hermeneutics is the most complex genre of applied Biblical interpretation. Though the doctrine of End Times is complex, all Christians agree that at the end of the New Covenant age, Jesus returns and vanquishes all His enemies, including death. We will speak in terms of generalities as not to divide over the most complex and controversial doctrine of the Christian Church, that is eschatology.

Psalm 2 - The Laughable Rebellion

Psalm 2 contains the broadest description of the overwhelming glorious triumph of Messiah over the power structures of the peoples and a warning to all governing authorities that have ever been to bend their will to the Messiah. Psalm 2 looks through the time/space continuum to a Day when the Messiah will rule, crowned with dominion, power, authority,

Eschatological Judgment

glory, and victory overall. This is an eschatological doctrine in its purest sense. While Christians may have different schemes on how this takes place, we all agree on the coming Messianic rule and reign of Jesus Christ at His Second Coming. Now, let's look at the movements in the text of Psalm 2 and explore the theological contrast of the Eschatological Judgment of God.

There are three movements in Psalm 2 that help us understand the nature of the Eschatological Judgment of God and these are:
1) The vanity of being rebellious towards God
2) Messianic promises that the Father has given the Son;
3) The promise that every earthly government will be submitted to the Son.

Most Christian theologians see an eschatological dimension in the New Covenant age that is a type of "first fruits" of the rule and reign of Jesus Christ as we preach the gospel, reap a harvest of souls, and expand the spiritual Kingdom of God. We would see Jesus' resurrection from the grave, His ascension, the proclamation of the gospel, and the spiritual authority of the Church as a fore-shadow of the ultimate eschatological event which is the second coming of Christ and His visible rule and reign in the earth. With this in mind, the Church stands as an eternal witness to the world and the spiritual principalities and powers that Jesus Christ is indeed the only Sovereign and Lord forever and ever, Amen.

The first movement in Psalm 2 covers verses 1-6 as it begins with, "Why do the nations rage and the people plot in vain?" These verses point to the reality that any resistance to the rule and reign of Christ is a futile endeavor. If one looks at the events that have unfolded in world history, we see that tyranny is always defeated, evil never prevails long term, and Christianity has prospered even under the worst persecutions. Psalm 2 teaches us that the Kingdom of God cannot be resisted and ultimately every person and government on the earth at any time, will be accountable to the Messiah. The attempt of the rulers of the earth to "burst their bonds" and "cast away their cords" is a laughable exercise in rebellion from God's perspective.

Not only is rebelling against the rule and reign of Jesus Christ laughable, but it is also terrifying because the fruit of this rebellion is the personal wrath of the Messiah towards His enemies at the end of the ages. Notice that both individuals and national governments are accountable to God. God's proof of the wrath to come is simply stated in Psalm 2:6, "I have set my King on Zion, my holy hill." There are many texts in the New Testament that describe the rule and reign of Jesus Christ as the fulfillment of Psalm 2. Here is a shortlist of them for further study: Acts 4:23-31; 13:32-33, 1 Cor. 15:20-28, Eph. 1:20-23, Phil. 2:9-10, Col. 2:12-15, and Heb. 1:13-14. These sections of Scripture teach us that Jesus is the Messiah prophesied in Psalm 2, and the New Covenant age is an intermediate age that will be completed when Jesus returns to rule and reign forever as a global King.

The second movement in Psalm 2 is the Messianic promises that God the Father has given God the Son in Psalm 2:7-9. The promise from the Father to the Son is the absolute rule and reign over all people. Psalm 2:9 is even more graphic with a Hebrew play on words that invokes a startling picture in our minds of Jesus breaking every ruler, resistor, and rebel by dashing them to pieces with His rod of iron. The text makes it clear: the rule and reign of Jesus cannot be resisted on account that it is God's sovereign decree to give the earth to the Second Adam and Davidic King, Jesus Christ, who has not only defeated Satan, but will defeat everything that is opposed to Him.

There is no escape for those who seek to flee or resist.

The third and last movement of Psalm 2:10-12 is the exhortation for all people and the governments that rule them to become obedient and submit to the Son. In these verses, we find a description of the four responses that God is offering to the world as it awaits the fullness of Jesus' coming Messianic rule and reign. The first response is for people to be wise and consider the warning that resistance and rebellion will not be a successful endeavor. The second response is to serve the Son with reverence and rejoice in being under the covering of the Messiah. The third response is to "Kiss the Son," which means "touch tenderly," in Hebrew. This is descriptive of relational worship and devotion that is experienced when people and nations turn their hearts toward Christ, and governments become accountable to God for the ways that they govern. The last, movement in the text is a promise that all who "take refuge" in the Son will be blessed, meaning there is a collective goodness that pours out on a nation that stays close to Him. It is the fruit of the Consequential and Forsaking Judgment of God that either brings blessings and favor, or withdrawal from God.

Psalm 2 reveals that the Eschatological

Judgment of God is a very real, terrifying, and fearful expectation for the rebellious, with both individual and national dimensions of accountability at the end of the New Covenant age. Though the Eschatological Judgment is a coming judgment, living with the knowledge that we and the nations we live in are accountable to the Eschatological Judgment of God, gives Christians the correct worldview and helps guide the course of our lives and the decisions we make every day. We could say that the Eschatological Judgment of God to come has a very real place in the hearts and minds of Christians and can be the fuel for Christian living and ministry action. The Eschatological Judgment of God has been the catalyst that has empowered Christians with the courage to stand in the face of persecution, the fuel that launches revival movements throughout the history of the Church, the passion that releases the personal love for Jesus in the hearts of His beloved, and the hope of eternal life.

Revelation 19 - The Glorious Coming

Revelation 19 is one of the most beautiful sections of Holy Scripture. It is ripe with worshipful declarations and glorious word pictures that frame the Eschatological Judgment of God as a wonderful event for the believer and a terrifying defeat for the rebellious. Because there are four schools of eschatological doctrine, we will not promote one over the other but speak in generalities that all Christians can agree upon. It is more important to see the bigger picture of the Eschatological Judgment of God than to divide over the diverse theological concepts concerning the how, when, and why of each school of eschatology. This book is concerned with only promoting how Christians should see the judgments of God.

Revelation 19 has two movements in that point our attention to the overarching themes of the coming rule and reign of Messiah, the future marriage of the Church to the Lamb, and the overwhelming and unstoppable destruction of the enemies of Christ at the end of the New Covenant era. In the first movement found in Rev. 19:1-10, we see the rejoiceful worship in heaven that results from Christ's victory over the fall of Babylon. In general terms, Babylon is an archetype for the world powers and the peoples who stand opposed to the rule and reign of Jesus Christ. Here, we see the multitudes of the redeemed crying out and worshiping Christ for His victory. They extol the glory of the Messiah, His judgments on the nations, and the eternal defeat of the rebellious who persecuted the Church and propagated sin throughout the nations of the earth. We finally see the justice of the Eschatological Judgment of Messiah has unfolded, coming into its fullness. These verses are a reflection and an invitation to worship Jesus, build hope for the future, and take comfort in the promise of His coming. Words will always fall short compared to the glory of God described in these verses. We could say the first ten verses of Revelation 19 sum up the entire Messianic victory of the Eschatological Judgment of God in Messiah, Jesus Christ.

Following the rejoicing of the saints in heaven, is the rejoicing of the twenty-four elders and the four living creatures as they agree with the joyful declarations of the saints that Jesus Christ is the Victor. There is an "Amen" and a "Hallelujah" from the court surrounding the throne. We see the beautiful antiphonal song of the saved, the bliss of the saints, the diversity of the spiritually created order singing, and declaring back and forth the praises of the Messiah's victory. It is a truly moving section of Scripture that invites our hearts to glory in Christ. The Eschatological Judgment of God is a glorious event and a wonderful day to behold for the beloved in Christ, as a voice from the throne declares praise to God. It is a positive event for those who believe in Jesus as our Savior because everything wrong in the world has been made right by Christ's victory over Babylon.

In Revelation 1:6-10 the voice of multitudes rejoice, worship, and declare that the wedding day of the Lamb has arrived and the Bride has made herself ready to consummate her marriage to the Lamb. In these verses, we see a faithful Church emerge across the time/space continuum that is mature, pure, and righteous. We should have hope for Christ's Church as the New Covenant era continues through the generations of believers who love God because Scripture gives us the promise that at some point the Church of Jesus Christ will have made herself ready to receive her Bridegroom God. We are told in verse 10 that these words are true, then ending with the beautiful declaration that "the testimony of Jesus is the spirit of prophecy." It is wonderful that the gospel prophesies the coming rule and reign of Jesus Christ. It is the glory and hope for the saved and the promise of destruction and defeat for the enemies of Christ. The Eschatological Judgment of God in Messiah is wonderful and fearful at the same time depending on which side of the spiritual war between Christ and His enemies a person or nation is on.

The second movement in Revelation 19:11-21 is the glorious metaphorical description of the coming of Christ to earth as heaven opens and Christ is riding a white horse to mete out judgment on His enemies. We have the most glorious description of Christus Victor in the text, such as Jesus wearing many crowns, His passionate eyes blazing like fire, His eternal Name, His robe dipped in blood, His Name, the Word of God, and many other metaphors and archetypes that describe His glory and power. I am writing with generalizations so as not to divide Christians along eschatological lines, however, we should have permission to have our hearts inflamed with love, hope, and joy in the coming Eschatological Judgment of Christ. What we are seeing in the text are word pictures that unfold the glorious revelation of the Messiah in the Eschatological Judgment of God that is coming on the earth.

Lastly, in Revelation 19:15 we see the use of parallel language that mirrors Psalm 2:9 where the sword that proceeds from Messiah's mouth strikes down the nations "with a rod of iron" and inaugurates His rule and reign over the power structures of the earth. As the glorious rule and reign of Christ are being established, an invitation for the birds that fly directly above to come and gorge themselves on the flesh of the kings of the earth gives us another fantastic word picture of the overwhelming defeat of all who are in open rebellion against

Messiah. The thought here is that though the power structures that stand against Christ and His Church seem to prevail through the ages, the Church can rest assured that all justice will be fulfilled when Messiah comes to rule and reign. There is much for more that could be written on this glorious section of Scripture, but for the sake of treading too far and offending brothers and sisters, we will end here with an invitation for each believer to seek God in His word concerning the mechanics of the coming of Christ at the end of the New Covenant age.

In summary, the Eschatological Judgment of God stands as a future event that plays through human history and culminates in the irresistible rule and reign of Jesus Christ, the Messiah. The New Covenant age is an era of God's mercy and forgiveness toward all who would say "yes" to Him in the good news of the gospel. Ultimately, the New Covenant era gives way to the Eschatological Judgment of Jesus that reveals Him as the true Lord of Lords and Kings of Kings. Wonderful anticipation for Christ's Church, and an awful reality for the rebels and power structures that resist Him. For Christians who live with the Eschatological Judgment of God in view, it motivates us to seek the lost, redeem the nations, and influence the seven movers of culture to honor Christ as we wait.

5

THE JUDGMENT OF HELL

The Judgment of Hell is the most terrifying of all the judgments of God because it is the irreversible and eternal judgment of the sinner. It is God's ultimate judgment that honors the choices that the sinner has made during their lifetimes. In Christian history, there have been three views of eternal judgment or the Judgment of Hell. These three views are Eternal Conscious Torment, Conditionalism, and Universalism. The Eternal Conscious Torment view of hell emerged in the 3rd Century AD as the most common view of Christians through the Middle Ages to the Reformation and is now the majority view in the Modern Era. The early

church father, Augustine, popularized the Eternal Conscious Torment view in his book, *The City of God*. Consequently, he holds the same view as most Christians. This view stands on three theological positions:
1) The souls of all people are immortal, whether they are sinners or saints.
2) Hell is the everlasting and eternal suffering and torment for the sinner.
3) The wages of sin are death. However, death is not understood in its natural meaning of the word, but death is a metaphor for the quality of life for the sinner in hell, a reality that ceases to be human and therefore is death.

The Conditionalist view of hell emerged early in Christian history, only to fade in the 3rd and 4th Centuries, and is now enjoying a resurgence in evangelical Christianity. The Conditionalist view stands on three theological positions:
1) Immortality of the soul is a gift from God and is only given when a person is in right relationship with God.
2) The wages of sin are death to the offender.
3) The fires of hell punish the sinner according to their degree of sin and will ultimately be burned out of existence.

The Judgment of Hell

This judgment is irreversible and eternal. This is a minority view but is being revisited by many evangelical Christians who wrestle with reconciling the goodness of God in the doctrine of hell or final judgment. Their argument for Conditionalism questions whether it is congruent with God's nature and character to punish a soul in eternal conscious torment for a limited lifetime of sin. There are metaphors in Scripture that describe the length of human life as "a vapor, a mist, a fading flower, or like grass." If Scripture describes human life in such temporal terms, then Conditionalists argue that the Eternal Conscious Torment of the sinner for 70-120 years of living is not congruent with the eternal, pure, good, and holy nature of God.

The Universalist view was popularized by the early church father Origen and has never been a majority view in historic Christianity. The Universalist view stands on three theological positions. These are:
1) All souls are immortal - saint or sinner.
2) Jesus' sacrifice on Calvary redeems every person's sin and saves them whether they have accepted Jesus' gift of salvation in the gospel or not.
3) The fires of hell are remedial in nature and every unbeliever will be "purified" by the fires of hell and eventually all

> people will bend the knee to Christ
> and be saved and live with Him
> eternally.

This view is not a majority view and faces many difficulties when trying to build a Biblical apologetic for it. I mention the Universalist view only for clarifying that these three views have existed throughout the long history of the Church and knowing about them helps us to develop or confirm our views of hell. Because of its Scriptural difficulties, Universalism will always be a minority view or even considered very unbiblical by serious seekers in God's Word.

The prospect of the Judgment of Hell is a doctrine that all Christians have considered when we reflect on the sacrificial death of Jesus on the cross. We believe that Jesus died on the cross as the only true, and one eternal sacrifice for sin and that the penalty of our sin was reconciled with God through that one act. Every Christian believes they are saved from the eternal judgment of hell by the blood of Christ and our trust in His sacrifice on the cross as the sacrifice that saves us from that fate. The Judgment of Hell is the personal accountability of the individual sinner to stand before a holy and perfect God, give an account of their lives, and receive the just penalty for their offenses against God's moral law in the light

The Judgment of Hell

of His Person. The Judgment of Hell reveals the goodness and grace of God as much as it reveals His justice. All of us look at the Judgment of Hell with hearts of gratitude knowing that we have been saved from this horrifying fate. The cross opens our hearts to the terrifying reality of hell because Jesus demonstrated the penalty of sin as He suffered on the cross. The metaphor for hell was revealed on the cross.

Regardless of our position on the Judgment of Hell, it is truly a sobering reality from which no one escapes. No humanist, atheist, or agnostic can escape their accountability to a holy Triune God. This is why Scripture says, "The fool says in his heart, 'There is no God.'" Now, let's explore the archetypes and metaphors for God's final judgment of the wicked.

Biblical Texts that Describe the Fate of the Wicked

The Scriptures describe a final and irreversible judgment of the wicked at the end of this world when all people are resurrected and give an account for their lives before God. Unfortunately, the Scriptures do not give specific details of what the final Judgment of Hell is exactly like. However, the Scriptures do give us enough information to determine what the nature of hell is in a general sense. Below we will look at the common Scriptural metaphors and archetypes that help us understand the serious and sobering final judgment of the wicked in hell.

Blown Away like Smoke and Melted like Wax

Psalm 68:1-2 describes the end of the wicked using the metaphor, "melted like wax." Psalm 68:1-2, "God shall arise, his enemies shall be scattered; those who hate him shall flee before him! As smoke is driven away, so you shall drive them away; as wax melts before the fire, so the wicked shall perish before God!"

Psalm 68:1-2 gives the reader various word pictures to teach us that rebellion against God is very serious and will end in a final inescapable way. Though the wicked flee from the presence of the Lord, they are blown away like smoke and melted like wax. These metaphors describe the end of the wicked and teach us that the wicked have no strength or ability to flee or resist, that they will be "like smoke, like wax that melts" and this judgment from God is final and permanent.

Consumed

One of the earliest metaphors for the final judgment of the wicked is found in Job 4:9 which reads, "By the breath of God they perish, and by the blast of his anger they

The Judgment of Hell

are consumed." Other texts using this same metaphor or archetype for the final judgment of the sinner are: Job 20:26, Psalm 104:35, Is. 1:28, and Jer. 9:16.

The Hebrew word for "consumed" is *kalah*, which can mean "come to an end, be ended, finished, be destroyed, be used up, exterminated, or fail." The Hebrew word for "consumed" does not give any detailed information on what "consumed" is exactly, but it does give us enough information to know that the final judgment of the wicked is permanent and irreversible. It invokes a feeling of sobering accountability to God as one considers that one cannot run away, escape, or preserve their own life in God's presence. The "breath of God", indicates that life comes from Him and every person is accountable to God for their lives. If a person is not pleasing to God, then they are "consumed," whatever that is. We only know that it cannot be escaped.

The Wicked Die

Another description of the end of the wicked is death. This description is used in both the Old Testament and the New Testament Scriptures. Let's explore Proverbs 11:19 and Romans 6:23 for more information. Other texts that use death as a description for the end of the sinner are Proverbs 19:16 and Isaiah 22:18.

Proverbs 11:19 - "Whoever is steadfast in righteousness will live, but he who pursues evil will die."

The Proverbs are beautiful compressed parables that impart to us deep truths for life in their contrasts. Hebrew parallelism is glorious because it is easy to memorize and it gives us wisdom that guides the course of our everyday lives. The movements in Proverbs 11:19 are simple. The righteous live and those who pursue evil die. The text does not say anything about how they die or the nature of the state of death, but only that the sinner dies. The Hebrew word for "die" in Proverbs 11:19 is *maveth*. It means "to die, death, dying, death personified, the realm of the dead, death by violence and death as a penalty." Though the text does not give us specifics on hell, it does teach us that the end of the sinner is death and not life; it's irreversible and final in its nature.

Romans 6:23 - "For the wages of sin is death, but the free gift of God is eternal life in Christ Jesus our Lord."

Romans 6:23 gives us two movements in the text that describe the end of the sinner. The first movement is that the payment for sin is death. The Greek word for "death" in the text is *thanatos*, which means "the death of the body, or separation of the soul from the body." The Strong's concordance expounds the definition to include "eternal conscious torment of the soul in the misery of hell," however, this definition of the word has been expounded by centuries of Christian tradition and not its etymology in Greek. The original use of the Greek word was simply "the death of the body." Romans 6:23 teaches us that death, whatever it is, depending on the position of hell we hold, is not life. It is the just and final payment for all of the sinful choices that a person has made throughout their lifetime.

The good news is that eternal life, or life that will always be, is a gift from God. It is a gift that is given to humanity in the Person of Jesus Christ. This is wonderful news for all people because though the wages of sin are death, eternal life is a gift that cannot be earned but only received. The contrast in the text is clear, sin leads to death, and life in Christ is a gift that is given by God to penitent sinners who exchange the death they earned by sin, for an eternal life they did not earn. This is the simplicity of the gospel and thrust of evangelistic endeavors, that Jesus died for the sinner and grants eternal life for those who believe. It is God's grace and not works from mankind that saves the soul from the corruption given to us in Adam. The wages of sin is death which is irreversible, irresistible, final, and permanent.

The Wicked are Blown Away like Chaff

In Psalm 35:5, we find another metaphor for the final judgment of the wicked. Psalm 35:5 - "Blow them away like chaff in the wind — a wind sent by the angel of the LORD." Other places in the Scriptures that use this word picture are Isaiah 29:5 and Hosea 13:3.

The metaphor of the wicked being blown away like chaff gives us very little detailed information concerning the final judgment other than the wicked will be removed like chaff is blown away by the wind. The imagery in the text teaches us that the wicked cannot resist the wind like chaff cannot resist the wind. They will be removed and not recovered. The metaphor leads us to believe that the end of the wicked is final, irresistible, and irreversible. Though we do not get details of the nature of the final judgment of God in hell, we do know that it is permanent.

Cut Off

One of the more common metaphors for the end of the wicked is that they are cut off. Some of the Scriptures that use this metaphor are Job 24:24, Psalm 75:10; 34:16, and Isaiah 29:20. Let's explore Job 24:24 and look at this metaphor in detail. Job 24:24 - "They are exalted a little while, and then are gone; they are brought low and gathered up like all others; they are cut off like the heads of grain."

There are several movements in the text that describe the end of the wicked. The first movement in the text is that the wicked only prosper for a short time. Their prosperity of perceived quality of life is not permanent but temporal. The second movement is that they are removed from the presence of the righteous. The third is that the wicked are humbled and have no strength to continue. The fourth movement in the text is that the wicked are gathered. The final fifth movement is that the wicked are cut off. The word for "cut off" in Hebrew is *namal* which means "to be circumcised, be clipped or cut off." Again, we do not get details on the nature of hell, however, we do know that the end of the wicked is irresistible, irreversible, and permanent in nature.

Burned like Chaff
John the Baptist described the end of the wicked as being burned up like chaff, adding to the Old Testament imagery that agrees with the idea of an irresistible, irreversible and permanent end of the wicked for their sinful and evil ways. These examples are found in

DIAKRINO: How Is God Judging the World Today?

Matthew 3:12 and Luke 3:17.

Matthew 3:12 - "His winnowing fork is in his hand, and he will clear his threshing floor and gather his wheat into the barn, but the chaff he will burn with unquenchable fire."

Luke 3:17 - "His winnowing fork is in his hand, to clear his threshing floor and to gather the wheat into his barn, but the chaff he will burn with unquenchable fire."

John's description of the end of the wicked adds a Messianic dimension to the final punishment of the wicked. "His winnowing fork" is an obvious reference to Jesus Christ who will stand as Judge of the living and the dead. Looking at the movements in the text, we see Jesus has the authority to judge the wicked since He holds the winnowing fork. We also see from this text that Jesus gathers the wheat. The wheat is what is good, therefore, Jesus gathers the righteous. Finally, we see the wicked are burned with a fire that cannot be quenched, a fire that cannot be put out, resisted, a fire that completely burns. John's description of the end of the wicked follows the Old Testament themes of the final punishment of the wicked and adds the Messianic dimension of Jesus, our Messiah, as the Judge who will execute the judgment of hell.

Where the Worm does not Die

Jesus taught about the end of the wicked in His teachings, so it is important to review what Jesus said about the final Judgment of Hell. Jesus is the Word of God, so the statements that Jesus makes and all His teachings are authoritative and must be believed. Jesus describes the end of the wicked, or hell, as a place where the worm does not die, a fire that burns, and a place of weeping and gnashing of teeth. In this section, we will examine these metaphors and expand the information we have about the Judgment of Hell.

Jesus quoted Isaiah 66:24 in His teachings on hell. This verse describes the end of the wicked at the end of the age. Isaiah writes, "And they shall go out and look on the dead bodies of the men who have rebelled against me. For their worm shall not die, their fire shall not be quenched, and they shall be an abhorrence to all flesh." Jesus affirms the prophet Isaiah and confirms the veracity of his prophecy of Scripture. It is important to see that Jesus never corrected the text of the Old Testament but affirmed it in every way. Jesus only corrected the misapplication of God's Word by the Sadducees and Pharisees.

Jesus also quotes this Isaiah verse in Mark 9:47-48 which reads, "And if your eye causes you to sin, tear it out. It is better for you to enter the kingdom of God with one eye than with two eyes to be thrown into hell, where their worm does not die and the fire is not quenched." For us to understand this verse, we need to consider the context of the culture in which Jesus was speaking. Jesus uses the Greek word *geena,* or *Gehenna,* the Hebrew word in the text. Gehenna is a metaphor for hell, or the archetype for the end of the wicked. It was the dump outside of Jerusalem where the carcasses of animals, trash, and the filth of the city were burned. It is located in the Valley of Hinnom, south of Jerusalem. Gehenna was the place that Isaiah was referencing in Isaiah 66:24, and it is the place that Jesus is referencing in Mark 47-48.

Gehenna, or Hinnom, was continually burning up the refuse, and the maggots were constantly feeding on the dead flesh. The imagery in the text shows that whatever is put in hell is consumed by fire and maggots. We learn that the wicked are like useless refuse which is gathered, burned and eaten by worms in the Valley of Hinnom, and that the end of the wicked is permanent, irresistible, and irreversible.

Weeping and Gnashing of Teeth
Another metaphor, or archetype, that

Jesus uses in the Gospels is "weeping and gnashing of teeth" to describe the end of the wicked. The Scriptures where Jesus uses this metaphor are: Matthew 8:12; 13:42; 13:50; 22:13; 24:51; 25:30, and Luke 13:28. The imagery of weeping and gnashing of teeth is a recurring theme of the end of the wicked and helps us expand our knowledge of the type of end that the wicked will suffer. Let's look at Luke 13:28 and Matthew 25:30 as examples of Jesus using the "weeping and gnashing of teeth" metaphor.

Luke 13:18 - "In that place, there will be weeping and gnashing of teeth, when you see Abraham and Isaac and Jacob and all the prophets in the kingdom of God but you yourselves cast out."

Matthew 25:30 - "And cast the worthless servant into the outer darkness. In that place, there will be weeping and gnashing of teeth."

The text in Luke describes a "place" and the text in Matthew describes that place as "outer darkness." The Greek words that describe the "outer darkness" that Jesus references are *exōteros skotos*. The literal meaning of these words is "outside darkness." *Skotos*, in Greek, is a metaphor for "being darkened in your thinking, under the influence of evil, or being devoid of the illuminating knowledge of God, or the light of God." The thought in the text is that the place where the wicked meet their end is a place devoid of the light of the Messiah, Jesus Christ. The response of the wicked in the place where they are judged is weeping, synonymous with regret, or gnashing of teeth, synonymous with anger and rebellion. We learn that the righteous are gathered and enjoy the presence of Jesus and the wicked are cast out from the illuminating presence of Jesus. Though we do not have definitive information regarding the nature of hell, we do know that the wicked cannot resist Messiah's judgment and that they either weep with regret or gnash their teeth in anger and rebellion at their end. Their end is irresistible, irreversible, and permanent in nature.

Sinners Die a Second Death

In Revelation 2:11 and Revelation 20:6, we are introduced to the "second death" that is associated with the final Judgment of Hell. This perhaps the most horrifying thought, that after the physical death of the body, there is a second death the sinner experiences that consummates their eternal judgment. Jesus gives us some insight into what the second death might be. In Matthew 8:22 and Luke 9:60, Jesus makes similar statements as He says, "Follow me, and leave the dead to bury

The Judgment of Hell

their own dead." This implies that people are already dead to eternal life apart from the Messiah. The exhortation from Jesus is that those who follow Him, have eternal life, and those who do not follow Him do not.

In Matthew 10:28, Jesus says, "And do not fear those who kill the body but cannot kill the soul. Rather fear him who can destroy both soul and body in hell (Gehenna)." Matthew 10:28 gives us more insight into the "second death" mentioned in Revelation 2:11 and 20:6. We must note here the word that is translated "hell" in Matthew 10:28 is the Hebrew word *Gehenna*, which we learned in previous verses is the metaphor and archetype of hell that emerges out of the imagery from the Valley of Hinnom in Isaiah 66:24, where the refuse and filth of Jerusalem is consumed by worms and consumed with fire. Jesus contrasts the persecutor who can kill a human body but cannot kill the soul, to God who can do both and, therefore, is worthy of reverence. The thought here is that believers should fear/reverence God and not fear or reverence anyone who takes a life. The contrast is clear: a mortal person can kill a body, God can destroy both body and soul in Gehenna. The Greek word for "destroy" is *apollymi*, which means "to destroy and entirely abolish."

Jesus does not give specific details on the exact nature of hell other than believers should reverence God and not human agencies that can kill bodies because God can destroy both the body and the soul. Again, we learn that hell, or Gehenna, is irresistible, irreversible, and permanent regarding the Judgment of Hell.

Now, let's look at the "second death" verses in Revelation and complete our study of the "second death" concept.

Revelation 2:11 - "He who has an ear, let him hear what the Spirit says to the churches. The one who conquers will not be hurt by the second death". The occasion for this statement by the risen Lord Jesus Christ concerns the Church at Smyrna. This Church was about to suffer more tribulation and persecution at the hands of Jews that were opposed to Messianic Christianity. The Jewish persecution was partnered with the local authorities who indeed persecuted many Christians. The early church father, Polycarp, was martyred in Smyrna. Jesus' exhortation is clear to the Church at Smyrna that Jesus knows their situation, more persecution is coming, and that overcoming this persecution will deliver them from a second death. Their body may die, but their soul will live and not die.

The next section of Scripture concerning the "second death" is Revelation 20:6 - "Blessed and holy is the one who shares in the first resurrection! Over such the second death has no power, but they will be priests of God and Christ, and they will reign with him for a thousand years."

In this passage, the first resurrection is mentioned. The first resurrection is being born again into the eternal life that we receive when we trust Jesus for the salvation of the soul and receive eternal life from Him. We were dead, but now we are alive. Ephesians 2:5 and Colossians 2:13 say that we were dead in our trespasses and sin, but now we have become alive together in Christ. Revelation 20:6 says that the second death has no power over those who share in the first resurrection, which is our born again experience in Christ.

The next movement in Revelation 20:6 is that believers are now priests of God and Christ. This is true as all believers are ministers of the gospel and all of us are qualified to minister to each other and to people because we are ambassadors of Jesus Christ. Rev. 20:6 concludes with a glorious promise of authority that was given to the Church as we reign with Jesus Christ. The "second death" is the eternal judgment of hell which is the irreversible and eternal judgment that unbelievers receive from God.

The Great White Throne and the Lake of Fire

In Revelation 20:11-15, we are introduced to the final judgment of saints and sinners. Some will go to eternal life because they are written in the Book of Life, and others who are written in other books will be thrown into the lake of fire. This is a day when everything is laid bare, all people are resurrected and all are judged before the Great White Throne. Death and Hades give up the dead who are sequestered there waiting to be judged according to what they have done. After everyone who has ever lived is judged, Death and Hades are thrown into the lake of fire. Revelation 20:14 states that "is the second death, the lake of fire". This is the end of the wicked, Death and Hades, the lake of fire.

While the Scripture is veiled regarding the exact nature of hell and does not explicitly say what it is like, Scripture is very clear that hell is final, permanent, irreversible, irresistible, and horrifying. Whether we hold the Eternal Conscious Torment position or the Conditionalist position of hell, it is clear that the Judgment of Hell belongs to a final day in the future, and in the gap of the New Covenant era, we are to preach the gospel, live for Christ, obey Him, serve Him and expand the Kingdom of God across all people groups in the world because the Judgment of Hell awaits.

What Happens to the Christian at Death?

As we conclude this chapter on the Judgment of Hell, it would be good to understand what the Scriptures say about what happens immediately after a Christian passes from this life to a life that will always be. The one place in Scripture where we find the most clarity on what happens to the Christian when they pass away is 2 Corinthians 5:6-8 which reads, "So we are always of good courage. We know that while we are at home in the body we are away from the Lord, for we walk by faith, not by sight. Yes, we are of good courage, and we would rather be away from the body and at home with the Lord." The Apostle Paul is convinced that when Christians die, they are present with Christ in conscious bliss. The other supporting text we can look at is Stephen's martyrdom in Acts 7:55-60 where Stephen sees Christ and prays, "Lord Jesus, receive my spirit." It seems that there is no time gap between Stephen's death and him being present with Christ in death.

There are many other supporting texts for the immediate conscious presence of the Christian being with Christ, like Revelation 6:9-10 where the souls of those who had been slain for their witness of Jesus Christ were crying out for vengeance and justice for the persecution they suffered. These souls are certainly alive and in the presence of God.

In addition to this text, Jesus teaches the parable of Lazarus the beggar and the rich man, in Luke 16:19-31, where Lazarus is being comforted, alive after physical death and the rich man is alive, while in torment. The Greek word for "torment" in the text is *basanos*, which means "a black siliceous stone (touchstone) that tests metal and is the metaphor for testing, torment, and discomfort." Jesus teaches us that the righteous are comforted in death and the unrighteous are tormented, tested, and in discomfort after death in this parable. Though the Bible doesn't explicitly say what happens to the sinner after death, this parable gives us the most information. It seems that the wicked are sequestered and waiting for the judgment of hell and are consciously aware of their impending punishment.

From this survey of Scripture, we can summarize that at the moment of death, the believer is comforted in God's presence and the sinner is in discomfort as they await the Judgment of Hell in a place called Hades. The human body decays and is wait-

The Judgment of Hell

ing for a resurrection of the dead body on the last day where it is reunited with the soul and spirit, then judged and thrown into the lake of fire, or in the case of Christians, raised and reunited with a resurrection body unto eternal life in Jesus Christ. See 1 Corinthians 15 for a detailed explanation of the type of body Christians receive at the resurrection of the dead in Christ.

6

HOW SHOULD CHRISTIANS SEE THE JUDGMENT OF GOD IN THE WORLD?

This abbreviated book has outlined the different types of judgment that are in Scripture. We learned that there are five expressions of judgment. They are Cataclysmic Judgment, Forsaking Judgment, Consequential Judgment, Eschatological Judgment, and the Judgment of Hell. Christians need to know what types of judgments of God are in the current world because our view of the judgment of God colors the way we see the current world events around us. To understand the judgment of God , is to know the grace and mercy of God. James 2:13 says that "mercy triumphs over judgment," and this is true. Christians should have hope for the future and the times in which God has appointed us to live because the Lord indeed is moving with mercy in the world before the Eschatological and Judgment of Hell to come.

This is especially important because there are many people today who look at the current events in the world and impute every large-scale catastrophe to the Cataclysmic Judgment of God. If we properly understand the Cataclysmic Judgment of God, we know that the archetype for that judgment of God has been fulfilled and belongs to an era in salvation history that has ended in the New Covenant era. This gives us comfort because we see God as a good God, and we see ourselves, the Church of Jesus Christ as the conduit of healing, reconciliation, and justice in the world. This is a wonderful freedom to experience, having hope for the future and a sense of mission that Jesus mandates and imparts to the Church. So much could be written about the glory, hope, and future of the Church, but words will always fall short of the eternal reality of the Kingdom of God in the world expressed through the Church.

How Should Christians See the Judgment of God in the World?

When we consider the Forsaking Judgment of God, we learned this is a judgment of God that is active in the world today. It is the collective agreement or disagreement between God and a people group. We learned that when a people group agrees with God, then God moves nearer to that nation. When a people group moves away from God, He honors their decision and the descending spiral of moral rot and corruption increases in the common culture. One only needs to look at the shell of Western Civilization to see the net gain result of a culture leaving God, embracing the idol of self and the worship of the human mind in Humanism. The good news is that the Church is the answer, the holy prescription for the sickness of society. Christians are mandated by Jesus Christ to preach the gospel, disciple nations, and preserve the illuminating knowledge of God in a culture where God blesses the nation and moves closer to its people. God is an authentic Lover who enjoys real relationship with His people. He is either moved closer to the people, or pushed away depending on how we honor Him as a people group. It is time for Christians all over the globe to be presently present in our culture for its blessing and benefit.

Another judgment of God which is also

active in the world today is the Consequential Judgment of God. We learned that this type of judgment is more personal in nature as we reap what we sow in the way we live our lives. If we sow to the goodness of God, then we reap blessing, favor, and eternal life. Not that we are saved by works, but that our good works flow from our relationship with God because we want to preserve our closeness to His Person. Scripture encourages all believers to persevere in faith and good deeds because they confirm the condition of our hearts. The Consequential Judgment of God is a judgment that is in play today, and the good news is that no matter what choices we have made, there is always the option of building a new future by repentance and aligning our hearts with God and, therefore, sow a new future that God can partner with.

We have been introduced to the Eschatological Judgment of God in Chapter 4. We reviewed Psalm 2 & Revelation 19, and from those Scriptures, we learned that the Eschatological Judgment of God belongs to an age to come after the New Covenant era. Though there are four main schools of end-time thought, they all agree that the Eschatological Judgment comes into fullness when Jesus Christ returns to earth as its

How Should Christians See the Judgment of God in the World?

revealed Messianic King who will conquer everything that opposes His rule and reign. The Church's role in the Eschatological Judgment of God is to fulfill our work of preaching the gospel, making disciples of nations, expanding the Kingdom of God, and spiritually preserve the knowledge of God as we occupy our nation and wait for Jesus.

Lastly, we learned about the terrifying and horrible end of the wicked in the Judgment of Hell which is final, irreversible, irresistible, and eternal in its nature. The Judgment of Hell is a sobering doctrine that should concern every Christian. It should move us towards compassion for the people around us since it is the destiny of all who do not accept the gift of salvation that the Father so lovingly provided in Jesus Christ. The Father gave the Son to die the death we all deserve, on the cross, for our sins. The Judgment of Hell should move us with mercy and soften our approach to a dead and dying world that is crying out for the new creation to emerge.

Diakrino was written to provoke Christians to believe that there is always hope for the world in the New Covenant age in which we live. The Forsaking and Consequential Judgments of God are reversible and Christians are the catalyst that initiates the redemption from death to life in people and the cultures in which they live. My prayer for you, the reader, is that you are now equipped with an easy-to-understand resource that has expanded your expectation for God's goodness in the world and encourages you to do your part in promoting His goodness. May God bless you in the journey as you co-labor with Him while being led by the Holy Spirit. In the age of the COVID-19 pandemic, or any other crisis in the fallen world that is subject to the corruption it inherited from Adam, Christians are the antidote to death, we are the light, the salt and we are ambassadors of a greater dominion, the Kingdom of God. May we all be motivated with the love of Christ and carry the good news of Jesus in the world.

Ut si uincent nos in nomine eius - May we conquer in His Name!

Resources

Helpful Resources for Further Study:

Dominion, How Kingdom Action Can Change the World - C. Peter Wagner

The Revelation of Hope - Rob Covell

The Fire that Consumes - Edward Fudge

Hell: God's Justice, God's Mercy: Rethinking the Traditional View of Eternal Torment - Dr. Harold R. Eberle

Spiritual Warfare Strategy - C. Peter Wagner

Note: All Bible verses are quoted from the English Standard Version

(Resource materials are available on Amazon)

Made in the USA
Las Vegas, NV
22 September 2021